IMAGES
of America

LATTER-DAY SAINTS IN
MESA

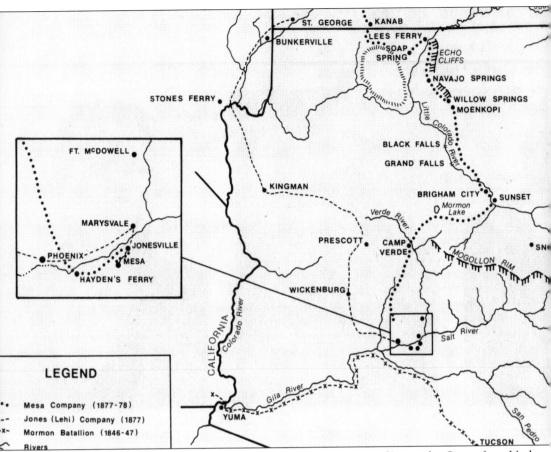

The settlement of Mesa began with the migration of two groups of Latter-day Saints from Utah. The Lehi Company (dashes) traveled from St. George in 1877, and the Mesa Company (dots) arrived from Salt Lake City and Idaho in 1878. Thirty years earlier, some of these settlers marched across southern Arizona with the Mormon Battalion. (Adapted from *Our Town*, 1978 edition.)

ON THE COVER: On Sunday, October 24, 1927, there began five days of dedication and preaching services, of concerts, dances, and dramas, to celebrate the completion of the Arizona Temple. The first presentation was a sunrise cantata, *The Vision* by Evans Stephens, sung by the Los Angeles–Hollywood Choirs. With choir members standing atop the annex, this photograph could also be the Monday evening "Grand Concert of All Choirs." (Mesa Arizona Temple.)

IMAGES
of America

LATTER-DAY SAINTS IN
MESA

D. L. Turner and Catherine H. Ellis

ARCADIA
PUBLISHING

Published by Arcadia Publishing
Charleston SC, Chicago IL, Portsmouth NH, San Francisco CA

Printed in the United States of America

Library of Congress Catalog Card Number: 2008932138

For all general information contact Arcadia Publishing at:
Telephone 843-853-2070
Fax 843-853-0044
E-mail sales@arcadiapublishing.com
For customer service and orders:
Toll-Free 1-888-313-2665

Visit us on the Internet at www.arcadiapublishing.com

To Floyd Lyman and LeOla Rogers Leavitt, whose love of Mesa and support helped make this work possible.

CONTENTS

ACKNOWLEDGMENTS

In 2007, the Mesa Historical Museum and the Southwest Museum of Natural History produced a book for Arcadia Publishing giving a broad overview of Mesa's history and diverse community. Jared Jackson, Arcadia's acquisition editor for the Southwest, thought a book on Latter-day Saints in Mesa would nicely complement Mesa's history. Our collaboration is the resulting product.

We express our appreciation for permission to use photographs from archival repositories in both Arizona and Utah. We are particularly grateful for the many photographs from the Mesa Historical Museum and the Mesa Arizona Temple. Additional photographs came from the Church of Jesus Christ of Latter-day Saints Archives (Church Archives), the Arizona Historical Society in Tucson (AHS/Tucson), Arizona State University Library Special Collections (ASU Library), Arizona State Archives in Phoenix, Utah State Historical Society, and Brigham Young University Library Special Collections (BYU Library). However, most photographs came from personal collections (as noted in the credit line at the end of each caption). Additional help came from the Anna K/Wagon Wheel Camp (Daughters of Utah Pioneers), ASU and Mesa Community College (MCC) Institutes of Religion, David Ellis, Joseph Fish, Virginia Fish, Owen Garner, Clark Huber, Lynette Madsen, Maricopa East Company (Daughters of Utah Pioneers), Starlyn Peterson, Mary Robson, Sharon Shields, Bernice Skinner, Olga Shill, Craig Smith, Jared Smith, Keith Teller, Anna V. Uremovich, Karina Wilhelm, and Tom Wright.

Because we include information from many unpublished sources, a traditional bibliography was inadequate in documenting our sources. However, we tried to cite these sources in the text. Two resources were particularly useful: Earl Merrill's books and Wanda LeBaron's writings. Original spelling and punctuation were retained with one exception. Because we used James W. LeSueur's "Autobiographical Notes," his typographical errors were corrected, abbreviations were spelled out, and minor punctuation was added. It should be noted that a few people mentioned in this book are not members of the LDS Church, but they may appear here as a result of the physical circumstances of the photograph.

This story of the Latter-day Saints in Mesa has been a joy to assemble.

INTRODUCTION

In 1875, Brigham Young sent a missionary/exploratory expedition of seven men from Salt Lake City, Utah, to Chihuahua, Mexico, under the leadership of Daniel Webster Jones. The entourage stopped in late November at Hayden's Ferry on the Salt River, and, ever on the watch for possible colonization sites, Jones broached the subject of Mormon settlement with Winchester Miller, a prominent valley rancher. Trained as a civil engineer, Miller thought the prime location for a ditch and colony would be farther up the Salt River in an area destined to become Lehi.

While the men were stopped at Tempe, one of the missionaries, Helaman Pratt, wrote home to his wives Victoria and Dora:

> Since writing to you before we have traveled about 100 miles, the country from the Verdy to this place is not very inviting, allthough some part would make good grasing. The Salt River Valley will average about 10 miles wide & it is 20 miles long, the land is of the best quality & watter enough to irigate every inch of it, the climate is very fine there being little or no winters, no snow, & ice only freases to the thickness of a windo pain. There is now about 1500 people located on the River, mostely Missirans. The leading men [particularly Charles Hayden] express a desier to have the Mormons come settle in this Valley. It is the opinion of the Brothren that there is suffisient land & water to sustain at least 10,000 inhabitants. There is about 5000 Pimas & Maricopa indians in this section of country, who are very peacable & industrious people they farm extensive on the Hila river 18 miles from hear.

After a 10-month journey, the men gave their report to Brigham Young. Some in the party were so impressed that they asked permission to immediately return. James Z. Stewart was one who started south again in October 1876. By early 1877, he was in Tempe and wrote back to Salt Lake: "A few days since, while riding out among the ruins near this place (Tampe, Maricopa Co., Arizona) the thought that a little account of them . . . might interest the readers of the *Instructor*, induced me to measure the largest one and make some inquiry concerning others."

Stewart first described his trip from Utah to central Arizona when he wrote that the ground "from the Big to the Little Colorado" was "strewn with pieces of pottery" and that the land had "the appearance of having been cultivated." He saw ruins high on the walls of a narrow canyon along the Little Colorado River, others along the Verde River, and numerous ruins in the Salt River Valley, "some of them very large." He then noted "two very large canals on the south and west sides of these ruins" and quoted Gov. Anson P. K. Stafford as saying, "The ruins of towns, farms and irrigating canals that are to be seen on every hand over this vast Territory, give abundant proof that this country was once densely inhabited, and that the people who lived here maintained themselves by cultivating the soil."

Information from both Stewart and Pratt piqued the interest of Utah Latter-day Saints. First, they were interested in missionary work among Native Americans, and second, they saw possibilities for new agricultural communities. Mormon colonization was ready to expand outside of Utah, and church leaders were open to the possibility of new towns in both Canada and Mexico. The Territory of Arizona lay between Salt Lake City and Mexico.

The first Mormon settlers along the Salt River, later known as the Lehi Company, arrived in 1877. They crossed the Colorado River at the west end of the Grand Canyon and traveled through the Mojave Desert. The next year, other settlers came from Bear Lake, Idaho, and Salt Lake City. They crossed at Lee's Ferry and became known as the Mesa Company. Additional groups arrived in the ensuing years; some of the people settled at Tempe (Nephi), others at Alma, Lehi, or Mesa.

Originally wanting to build agricultural-based communities, the pioneers also became freighters, miners, teachers, and businessmen. They greatly benefited from the construction of Roosevelt Dam and other irrigation projects, both with income from construction services and from the more consistent water provided by the dams and canals. They raised hay and bees, fruits and vegetables, milk and beef. But most importantly, they raised large, faithful families who continued to build up both their church and their community. Today the Mesa area has the largest population of Latter-day Saints in Arizona.

Members of the Church of Jesus Christ of Latter-day Saints have traditionally been a people of monument building and commemorations. On February 14, 1956, several hundred people gathered at 526 East Main Street in Mesa's Pioneer Park to witness the dedication of Elvin White's *Mural in Stone*. Built of red sandstone and granite, and acknowledged to be one of the most original creations in the West, this rustic memorial was designed to honor the Mormon pioneers who founded the Lehi and Mesa areas.

Dedicated on the anniversary of the arrival of the Mesa Company in Jonesville (later Lehi), White's creation uses symbolism to remind everyone of the events that led to the phenomenal growth of Latter-day Saints in the Salt River Valley. Within the mural is a rugged outline representing the surrounding mountains crossed by early settlers. A wagon wheel represents their primary mode of transportation. A chimney, roof, and window signify settlement, shelter, and culture; a stone bench represents recreation and rest. The incorporation of water through a small waterfall suggests the canals and irrigation from the nearby river leading to an agricultural heritage.

The park and monument also commemorate pioneer activities directly tied to the contributions and influence of indigenous Native Americans. Early Mormon farmers simply enlarged ancient Hohokam irrigation canals to carry water to their crops. Local Pimas (*Akimel Au-Authm*, River People) and Maricopas (*Xalychidom Piipaash*, People who live toward the water) assisted with much-needed labor and provided sustenance to early Latter-day Saints.

Pioneer Park and White's monument are located across the street from the Mesa, Arizona, Temple. Completed in 1927, the temple has served Latter-day Saints across the entire state for 80 years. The temple itself reminds Latter-day Saints of the sacrifices the early settlers made coming to the desert. The temple is beloved by all, who feel the peaceful influence within its walls and enjoy the blessings of the many marriages performed there.

Today the efforts of these early arrivals may seem obscured at times with the bustling labyrinth of highways and shopping malls. However, evidence of Latter-day Saint settlers and their contributions may still be found within the surrounding communities. It can be seen in the names of streets, parks, schools, and churches. It can be seen within the present-day civic and social institutions. It can be felt within the community atmosphere and traditions. Indeed, the influence of these early Latter-day Saints has not been forgotten. This is their story—their mural in print and photographs.

One

LEHI AND THE MESA COMPANY

Migration, whether by bird or human, whether each spring and fall or but once in a lifetime, requires crossing physical barriers such as a mountain or desert, canyon or ocean. The Grand Canyon and the Colorado River was that barrier to colonization of Arizona by members of the Church of Jesus Christ of Latter-day Saints living in Utah and Idaho.

The earliest ford above the Grand Canyon was at El Vado de los Padres, or Crossing of the Fathers, 35 miles upstream from the mouth of the Paria River. Natural steps down to the north side of the river could be negotiated by horses, but not by wagons, so an alternate crossing was sought. Downriver, 200 miles through the Grand Canyon, ferries were established at the mouths of the Grand Wash and the Virgin River.

However, the most important crossing was Lee's Ferry at the mouth of the Paria River. The first successful crossing here was in 1864 with a raft constructed by Jacob Hamblin. The most unique crossing was in January 1878, when several prospective settlers found ice thick enough for wagons to cross one at a time. Anthony W. Ivins wrote, "The river was frozen from shore to shore, but, above and below for a short distance, the river was open and running rapidly." It is believed this was the only crossing on ice.

The Lee's Ferry route became so important to Arizona couples traveling to the St. George Temple that Will Barnes nicknamed this the Honeymoon Trail. A monument erected by Juanita Brooks and other John D. Lee descendants in 1961 rightly proclaimed this crossing as the "northern gateway to Arizona for 54 years—from 1873 to 1927" and stated, "this ferry made possible the colonization of Arizona."

Brigham Young has been called the American Moses and is particularly well known for his colonization of the West. He died in 1877 and, in the last years of his life, sent families to Arizona—to the Little Colorado, Salt, San Pedro, and Gila Rivers. President Young (seated center with top hat) visited the confluence of the Virgin and Colorado Rivers on March 17, 1870. (BYU Library MSS.P-24-722.)

Five of the men Brigham Young called as the "First Expedition into Mexico" in 1875 are, from left to right, (first row) Helaman Pratt, Daniel Webster Jones, and James Stewart; (second row) Wiley Jones and Anthony Ivins. Head of the expedition, Daniel Jones fought as a Missouri Volunteer during the Mexican War and, after his discharge, remained in Chihuahua for two years. He became fluent in Spanish, which he later used to good advantage. (Utah Historical Society P.2 10034.)

SON
DANI

These men founded Colorado River ferries. (1) In 1873, at the mouth of the Paria River, John Blythe constructed a 20-by-40-foot barge that could hold two teams and loaded wagons. The Mesa Company used this crossing (Lee's Ferry). A "typical boat" (below) was used until 1929 when the Navajo Bridge was completed. (2) Below the Grand Canyon, Harrison Pearce established a ferry at Grand Wash in 1876; Bishop John Hunt of Snowflake entered Arizona here. (3) Daniel Bonelli operated a ferry where the Virgin River meets the Colorado (near and sometimes called Stone's Ferry); the Lehi Company crossed at Stone's Ferry, with Joseph McRae reportedly paying $10 per wagon. (4) Anson Call's ferry at the mouth of the Las Vegas Wash was important because church leaders hoped steamboats could be used for emigrants. (Church Archives; right P2913-2, below P7145-1.)

With Jones's favorable report, Brigham Young issued calls to 13 families at an October 1876 conference. In January, the Jones, Merrill, Rogers, Steele, Biggs, Brady, McRae, Turley, and Williams families were ready to leave St. George, and Young personally came to see them off. They traveled with no oxen, reached the Salt River in 44 days, and made dry camp nine times. Isaac Turley (above with family in 1878) was wagon master. (Wanda Smith.)

When Daniel Jones and Henry Rogers expressed concerns as they planned the expedition, Brigham Young promised they would be inspired to know where to stop. Rogers envisioned a river bottom with cottonwoods, an adobe hut, and a man with a wide-brimmed hat.

On March 6, the company, reaching the McDowell ford, stopped for their noon meal. In the distance, Rogers saw his vision confirmed. (Painting by Wilford Biggs.)

The new arrivals found a few Native Americans already living along the Salt River. Although none could speak English, some could speak Spanish. Therefore, Jones initially handled all interactions between the two groups. Incarnacion Valenzuela, a man who was both Tohono O'Odham (Papago) and Spanish, became their interpreter. Valenzuela traveled with the missionaries throughout southern Arizona. Claudina Wood said, "Grandfather [Valenzuela] was listening all the time and trying to feel the message of the gospel." He was baptized in 1884. Above, Edward Curtis photographed these Maricopas gathering saguaro fruit in handwoven baskets about 1906. Right, Incarnacion Valenzuela (center, with necktie) is pictured with his wife, Sarah, and some of his children and grandchildren about 1912. (Above Library of Congress; left Church Archives P4451:3.)

Probably the first church members to enter Arizona were Mormon Battalion soldiers who, in December 1846, marched east to west passing through Tucson. Future Mesa resident Henry Standage kept a journal. The battalion members ate Pima watermelons on Christmas Day and gathered mesquite beans for food. Thirty years later, another of these men who returned was Philemon Merrill. Suffering through the heat of a Mesa summer and remembering the lush grasslands on the San Pedro (compared to Mesa), in August 1877, Merrill convinced about half of the Lehi contingent to move farther south and established the town of St. David. Other Mormon Battalion members settling in the Mesa area included William Maxwell (left), George Dykes (below with wife Julia), Henry Brizzee, Schuler Hulett, William Johnstun, William Prows, George Steele, and Samuel Thompson. (Left Mesa Historical Museum; below Arizona State Archives 97-8324.)

The Crismon, Sirrine, Pomeroy, Robson, Mallory, Schwarz, and Newell families from Paris, Idaho, and Salt Lake City, later known as the Mesa Company, traveled south with 25 wagons, 16 span of horses and mules, 29 yoke of oxen, about 60 loose horses, and about 200 milk cows and beeves. The loose cattle and horses were herded ahead of the wagons by teenage boys, and although vital to the Arizona community, the animals made travel slow (five months). Above, C. W. Carter photographed Mormon pioneers in southern Utah about 1873. Note telegraph poles, which were installed at Pipe Springs in 1871 (versus 1873 in Phoenix). Below, Arizona historian James McClintock listed these three men (from left to right, Charles Crismon, Francis Pomeroy, and George Sirrine) as "Founders of Mesa." (Above ASU Libraries CP SPC 41:2; below Church Archives P2913:2.)

Esther Crismon Sirrine, wife of George Sirrine, traveled to Arizona with the Mesa Company in 1877. This photograph with her sons George (left) and Warren was probably taken in San Bernardino, California, about 1856. Enduring a 2- to 3-foot 1877 Christmas Eve snowstorm between Mormon Lake and the Verde Valley, Esther's last child, Florence, was born a few days later. Three babies were born on the trip to Arizona. (Church Archives P4008.)

Earl Merrill blamed the "heat and hardships of that first summer on the river" for three deaths. Caroline LeSueur Mallory and her baby daughter died in July, and four-year-old Marian Belle Schwarz died in October. Weeden Vander Hakes (right), who died in 1884, was the first burial in the Mesa Cemetery. (Mesa Historical Museum.)

To earn a living for their families, early Latter-day Saints in Mesa frequently pursued a variety of vocations in addition to farming. Freighting, mining, and brick making were particularly important. Freighting was the earliest to prove profitable as arriving settlers had ready teams and wagons. A growing population, nearby military fort, developing mining districts, and water reclamation projects demanded delivery of goods and supplies. (Mesa Historical Museum.)

Justus Morse, Collins Hakes, and brothers Orrin and Orlando Merrill discovered gold on the western slope of the Superstition Mountains in 1892. They later sold their claim to a large mining interest out of Denver, and the town of Goldfield sprang up by fall 1893. Although the area produced high-grade ore, the mines played out by 1898. Today Goldfield survives as a popular tourist destination (above). (Robert Schoose.)

Using the remnants of ancient Hohokam canals, and with help from Native Americans living in the area, Latter-day Saint settlers immediately began a canal to divert water from the Salt River to land that could be cultivated. This canal was used for 13 years until Dr. A. J. Chandler, with his steam-powered dredges, expanded and renamed it the Consolidated Canal. However, it was not until the completion of Roosevelt Dam that an adequate, consistent water supply made

Edward Curtis photographed this Maricopa woman dipping water from a canal/ditch in 1906. Although the canals and ditches could be treacherous during flooding and high water, they also were popular spots for swimming, fishing, and picnicking. (Library of Congress.)

large-scale agriculture possible. This wide-angle view of four canals in Mesa was produced by the California Panorama Company about 1908. Note the cottonwood trees that grew on the banks of the canals until 1924, when concrete began to be used to line the canals to prevent seepage. (Library of Congress.)

Leslie Brewer is here at the headgates. He recalled swimming three times a day to stay cool and stated, "We loved to fish, sometimes with a hook and line, but more often not. When the water would be cut down to six inches deep, we would spear the fish with a pitchfork. When we had a tub full, we would take them down to the Mexican district and sell 'pescado fresco.'" (Lucille Kempton.)

The 1908 *Phoenix Gazette* reported, "Granite Reef camp will soon be a thing of the past, but it will go down in history as one of the best regulated and most sanitary camps in the territory. The men have enjoyed the luxury of a daily mail service, electric lights, a complete system of waterworks with showerbaths in connection, private tents with concrete floors, and many other conveniences." With Red Mountain in the background, the partially completed dam can be seen

This 20-mule team is on the Apache Trail at the top of Fish Creek Hill. With the completion of Roosevelt Dam and the massive storage lake, Mesa farmers no longer had to worry about periodic droughts common to the Southwest, and Mesa agriculture expanded. Orley Seymour "O. S." Stapley spoke at the dedication ceremonies of the dam, as did Pres. Theodore Roosevelt, for whom the dam was named. (ASU Libraries MCL.34966.M3.)

here between derricks on either side of the river. When completed, the Granite Reef diversion dam turned the entire flow of the Salt and Verde Rivers into irrigation canals. Many Mesa residents came to the dedication; the dam was valued by "not only the farmers but by every merchant, businessman, and everyone else." (Library of Congress.)

Joseph W. Bond was one of the teamsters who worked on Roosevelt Dam; he was always proud of his team of horses. He is pictured here with grandchildren Dorris, Dortha, and William "Billy" Bond in front of the family home on the southwest corner of Country Club and University Drives. (Kenneth Bond.)

In 1889, Hubert H. Bancroft described the Salt River Valley and wrote, "By canals that have been and are being constructed, large areas of the desert are being transformed into grain-fields, orchards, vineyards, and gardens. . . . Here is one of the Pima Indian reservations, and here the Mormons have their most prosperous settlements." The farm of Alexander Findley MacDonald, president of the Maricopa Stake in 1882, was illustrated in the above lithograph from 1884. The Relief Society hall, hotel, and store (right) were the beginning of Mesa. (Andrew Wallace's *The Image of Arizona*.)

At left is a photograph of Alexander Findley MacDonald taken in Phoenix in the mid-1880s. MacDonald was a colonizer who helped build the communities of Provo/Springville and St. George/Middleton in Utah, Mesa, and then Colonias Juarez, Garcia, and Dublán in Mexico. (Church Archives P1700:3267.)

Charles Hopkins Allen (age 91, right) was born in New York in 1830 and moved with Mormon migrations from Kirtland to Nauvoo to Provo to California to Cache Valley and finally, seeking relief from rheumatism, to Mesa in 1882. He served as the director of the Mesa Canal Company, was a missionary on the Gila and Salt River Reservations, and was ordained a Patriarch in 1912. (Barbara Nielsen.)

Before combines, wheat was cut (headed) when dry and hauled to the threshing machine. Joseph Clark was farming 800 acres in Lehi in 1898. These men include, from left to right, Benjamin Noble with four horses driving the header, Joseph Clark on the header elevator, Dudley Jones driving a header bed, Joe Garcia and Will Jones on the stack, and Joseph Noble driving the second header bed. (Kenneth Noble.)

Additional settlers came to Mesa a few at a time. The adobe house above is the Hyrum Phelps home. Houses progressed from wagon beds, boweries, and tents to adobe and then lumber and brick. On December 7, 1882, Wilford Woodruff wrote to Benjamin F. Johnson (below with two of his wives), "I hope you will get a settlement in some part of the country that will suit you and be a benefit to you. Most of the people speak highly of the Salt River country. I expect it is quite warm in mid summer." Johnson was a successful Utah businessman, but by 1887, over 300 members of his family had settled in the Salt River Valley. This is considered the largest relocation effort of any single extended family to Arizona. (Above Barbara Nielsen; below BYU Library P230.)

James W. LeSueur came with his family to Mesa in 1879 as a six-month-old child. The family, however, moved to St. Johns after about a year, as LeSueur wrote, "on account of the heat." LeSueur moved back to Mesa in 1906, buying and selling businesses and property, including this store. A 1920 fire in the store left him with "debts galore," which he eventually paid off. (Lee Peterson.)

Countless LDS men helped build the city of Mesa. The newspaper wrote of Joseph W. Clark, "Mr. Clark's civic works—for which he either subscribed or helped organize—include the high school building, the ice plant and a dairy business, the experimental farm, the gas plant, a telephone system, furniture and hardware business and the Clark addition to Mesa." At right is Mesa's gas plant. (Annette Shumway.)

ONE OF THE FIRST TRUCKS MADE BY THE I.H. Co. 1908 ~ O. S. STAPLEY ~

O. S. Stapley came to Arizona in 1882 at age 16. He immediately began work as a farm hand, then became a stage driver, and finally in 1893 was hired by the Kemp hardware store. By 1895, the store failed, and Stapley purchased the company with his father-in-law, Alexander Hunsaker. Thus began the O. S. Stapley Company, which served Salt River Valley farmers with Sherwin-Williams paints and F. E. Meyers pumps for more than 75 years. In 1908, Stapley sold two of these International Harvester trucks (above) to J. H. Norton to transport passengers and freight to Roosevelt. In 1911, Stapley purchased three stagecoaches (below) that used a unique leather suspension, making the coach sway forward and back rather than sideways. It was designed to carry 12 passengers and was used here in a 1977 parade. (Above ASU Special Collections CP.RD.50; below Mesa Historical Museum.)

International Harvester and O. S. Stapley signed a contract in 1916, which meant Stapley Hardware became one of the oldest IH dealerships in the West. The contract stipulated that Stapley open stores in Glendale and Phoenix, which he did in 1917 and 1919 respectively. Above is a row of IH tractors ready for Salt River Valley farmers. (ASU Special Collections CP.MCL.97195.A3.)

Civic involvement has been important for LDS members. In 1893, Mabel Ann Hakes (seated above with her husband, Collins, and children) represented Mesa at the Chicago Woman's Suffrage Convention. An irate gentleman stated that women should be home sewing buttons on shirts and darning their husbands' socks. She quietly responded that he would be pleased to know all the buttons were sewn and socks darned before she left home. (Glynna Reinsch.)

Mont and Frank Vance were born in 1885, twin sons born of early Mesa pioneers John and Sarah Vance. They were always close, and in 1903, they were married on the same day (to Winnifred Richins and Vera Burton respectively). By 1910, Mont was working in a creamery, and Frank was working as a carpenter. Shortly after this, they opened a store and bakery next to the O. S. Stapley Hardware Store (above). The photograph below shows, from left to right, Mont Vance, Robert Burton, and Alex Petrie wrapping bread about 1920. Later they opened stores in Globe and Phoenix. The Phoenix store later became the Rainbo bakery. (Both Mesa Historical Museum.)

Other Latter-day Saint–owned businesses sprang up in Mesa and the surrounding communities. Pictured above is Loren Vaughn Guthrie with his daughter Norma at the Old Arizona Land Company, a real estate office in Mesa. Guthrie was in business with Hank Cummard until 1921, when the partnership was dissolved. (Jeanne Wright.)

In a bygone era when dry cleaning and laundry was picked up and delivered to your door, Joseph A. Ball drove a laundry truck in Mesa, here pictured with the Willis Laundry and Linen Supply truck. Ball also drove for the Maricopa and the Spic 'n' Span Laundries. (Kenneth Bond.)

Almost all men in Mesa's Company D, National Guard of Arizona, were Latter-day Saints. The photograph above is at Morenci in 1902 when the guard was called to quell riots at the mines. Joseph Noble enlisted in the National Guard in 1908 and became captain of Company D in 1913. (Another Latter-day Saint, Edwin LeBaron, was concurrently captain of Tempe's Company C.) Noble encouraged Snowflake's short-lived Company F by combining it with Company D at the 1913 Prescott encampment and by visiting Snowflake. The *Snowflake Herald* reported that he "assured the home company that their drill was improving and congratulated the men on their fine appearance and spirit." Below, Joseph Noble is seated (center) with the Arizona Rifle Team at national matches in Jacksonville, Florida, in 1914. (Above AHS/Tucson PC005; below Kenneth Noble.)

After the 1914 summer encampment at Camp Huachuca, Arizona, Adj. Gen. Charles Harris expressed pleasure with the men's "knowledge of camping and their ability to march." However, he noted, "the weakness of our organization was shown in preliminary armory drill and instruction, and as I have stated before, we must have armories to correct this defect." Mesa's armory (above) was built in 1921. (Mesa Historical Museum.)

When long-strained relations between the U.S. government and various factions in Mexico erupted in 1916, Pres. Woodrow Wilson mobilized the National Guard. The 1st Arizona Infantry arrived at Douglas on May 12–13, 1916. Approximately 74 Mesa men served on the border for a year, then many were inducted into the 158th Infantry and sent to France. Officers (including Joseph Noble) are shown here at Naco, Arizona, in 1917. (Kenneth Noble.)

Many outstanding Latter-day Saint families have contributed to the growth of both the church and the community. One example is the Lorenzo "Lo" and Theresa Wright family. In 1928, Wright was appointed to serve a two-year term as the warden of the state penitentiary. While there, he oversaw improvements to the prison as well as the execution of Eva Dugan, the only woman ever hanged in Florence. Pictured here are Lo and Theresa with children, from left to right, Margaret, Bassett, LaVaughn, Tom, Jack, and Bill (and Bob, the dog). Both Lo Wright and his son Harold served as Maricopa Stake presidents, with Harold eventually becoming temple president and regional representative. (Both Jeanne Wright.)

Lo Wright (right) moved his family to Mesa in 1932. They opened a grocery store, in part with money saved by Theresa from the sale of chickens. The family's holdings soon expanded to include stores in Chandler, Velda Rose, Tempe, and Queen Creek and included Jack's Wholesale Food Outlet, APG Market, Jack's Cost Plus 10%, and Jack's West End. Below, Jack Wright works at the family store as a young man (shown here with his trademark smile). The Wrights sold their business in 1981. (Both Jeanne Wright.)

When the Phelps family opened their Cost Plus 10 Market in 1957, the grand opening included the normal free groceries (one basket every 30 minutes), potted plants, orchids for the ladies, balloons for kids, cake, chocolate milk, snow cones, popcorn, and ice cream. They also gave away a Highpoint freezer and a German shepherd puppy, a "descendant of the famous Rin Tin Tin." (Stephen Phelps.)

Milano Music has been providing music instruction and selling sheet music and instruments to Mesa residents for 60 years. Shown above are, from left to right, Mila, Cene, Frank, Elma, Laura, and Henri Milano in 1955. Elma Milano was an accomplished accordionist, as was her grandmother Barbara Allen, who formed the Granny Band. Elma gradually expanded her store; it is now run by second- and third-generation family members. (Mila Linton.)

In 1919, Sreeve Peterson began Peterson Brothers' Gas Station on Main Street (above) with his brother Bill. The gas station became famous among Mesa children for having the coldest drinking water in town, freely dispensed. Peterson later bought out his brother and expanded the business to include a sporting goods store. As part of this business venture, he sponsored an annual deer hunting contest, giving away a free rifle to the hunter bringing in the first buck of the season. Encouraged by church directives promoting home beautification and gardening, Peterson became renowned for the beautiful flowers he planted annually in his front yard. (Both Lee Peterson.)

Harold Dana represents the many Latter-day Saints who serve as public safety officials in Mesa. During the early 1940s, Dana was assigned to Mesa as the area Maricopa County sheriff deputy. He organized the Junior Sheriff Safety Patrol (Dana is seated above at Alma School), a program that trained elementary school children to oversee school crossings before and after school and at recesses. Dana later joined the Mesa police force as a motorcycle patrolman and is shown below providing comfort and a soda to 18-month-old Freddie Stockett, who was found walking across Main Street alone on May 7, 1953. The parents, Mr. and Mrs. Turner Stockett, were relieved with the return of their child. (Both Nancy Norton.)

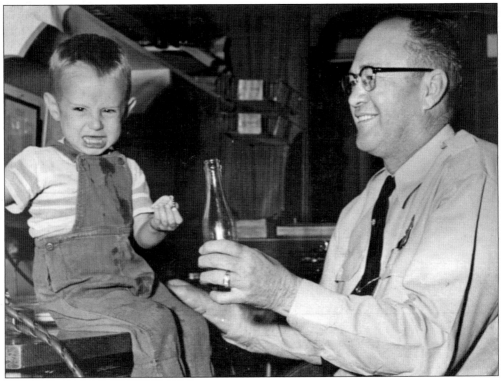

Latter-day Saint veterinarians in the Salt River Valley included Marion Smith and Ray Russell. Smith (far right) graduated from Texas A&M, helped found the Phoenix Zoo, and served as a veterinarian and board member for 25 years. He is shown here in 1969 with animal trainer Paul Fritz (left) and veterinarian Howell Hood helping extract an African lion's abscessed tooth. (Wanda Smith.)

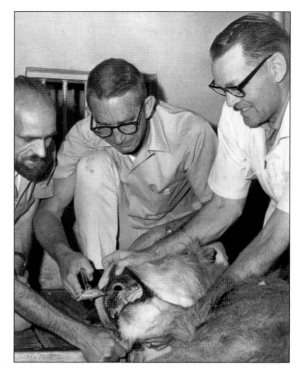

Ray Russell graduated from veterinary school at Kansas State and returned to establish a practice on Country Club Drive. Active in Scouting and church leadership, he used this card during his unsuccessful 1982 run for Congress (against John McCain). Written on the back of the card is, "Like Congressman John Rhodes, Ray Russell is *above* politics. Like John Rhodes, Ray Russell is a natural-born leader." (Ray Russell.)

In 1967, Gov. George Romney of Michigan announced his candidacy for president of the United States. Born in Colonia Dublán, Mexico, and with Mesa's ties to the Mormon colonies in Chihuahua, he could count on most of the vote from Mesa. Here retirees at Dreamland Villa in east Mesa celebrate Romney's candidacy and his birthday, July 8, 1967. Romney was later secretary of Housing and Urban Development. (Photograph by Dale Welker; courtesy Dilworth Brinton Jr.)

Louis Stradling, a Mesa resident since 1930 and part owner of Stradling's Fine Cabinetry, will be remembered by many as the man who started Constitution Week. Stradling requested that Sen. Orrin G. Hatch petition Pres. Ronald Reagan to set aside the week surrounding September 17 as a time to celebrate the signing of the constitution and Citizenship Day. Stradling is shown here (fourth from left) at Williams Field during World War II. (Louis Stradling.)

Dilworth Brinton was active in a variety of civic organizations and became famous around Mesa for turning out delicious Dutch oven rolls. Learning to mix yeast bread from his mother, he adapted the recipe to make his Dutch oven rolls, which, in 1962, were highlighted in *Boys' Life*. It was estimated at one time that more than $50,000 was raised for various community and church projects from Brinton's Dutch oven dinners and barbecues. Below, Brinton is serving Sen. Barry Goldwater at a John Rhodes "Meet the Candidate" barbecue in 1976. (Both photographs by Dale Welker; courtesy Dilworth Brinton Jr.)

In November 1941, the Henry Standage Camp of the Daughters of Utah Pioneers was organized for women in the Alma District of Mesa with Ethel Russell as captain. DUP members collected pioneer stories, journals, relics, and artifacts to honor ancestors. Russell is shown here with the DUP monument in 1956; dressing in pioneer costume for camp meetings was encouraged. (Ray Russell.)

The Shill family arrived in 1880. They farmed, and the boys worked in the Lehi brickyards. A local legend that Miguel Ortega, an itinerant sheepherder, found gold in northern Maricopa County inspired Milo to go prospecting with Frank Shill, Frank Biggs, and Lawrence Ellsworth. The youths searched much of the Cave Creek area but never found gold. In this photograph of the Shill brothers, believed to date after 1940, are, from left to right, (seated) Orson and Wright; (standing) Otto, Scott, Frank, and Ralph. (Alice and Pat Boyle.)

Lehi residents marked their centennial anniversary with an extensive reenactment of the 425-mile trek from St. George to Lehi. The modern trek was all on horseback; it began on February 12, 1977, and ended February 28 in time for the parade down Main Street in Mesa. Periodically some or all of this reenactment has been repeated. In 1994, Leon C. Jones, a descendant of Daniel W. Jones, led the group again from St. George to Mesa, but this time with wagons. Some of the route had to be modified because of private land issues, but the wagons are seen below passing the citrus trees of Lehi/Mesa. (Both Alice and Pat Boyle.)

Regardless of all business, church, and community involvement, Latter-day Saint colonization in Mesa and other parts of Arizona was really about families. At left is a baby picture of Carol Biggs, daughter of Wilford Biggs and Detta Lisonbee, born in 1923. Below are twins, Dorris and Dortha Bond, daughters of Joseph Bond Jr. and Florence Ellsworth, born in 1920. Included in the 1946 *Primary Children's Songbook* was Bertha Kleinman's poem, "I Have Two Little Hands." It was (and is) used to teach "That children can only be happy all day, When two little hands have learned how to obey." In 1915, the church began encouraging families to hold "Family Home Evening," now on Monday nights, to better teach gospel principles to children. (Left Zena Hunt; below Kenneth Bond.)

Two

IN PURSUIT
OF EDUCATION

Education has always been emphasized within the Church of Jesus Christ of Latter-day Saints. Brigham Young stated, "A good school teacher is one of the most essential members in society." Holding to New England principles of hard work, and despite the demands of an agricultural-based economy, education was not forgotten in early Mormon settlements. Schools were held in any available space, and children were required to attend unless needed for garden and fieldwork.

Settlers petitioned for a school district in Lehi sometime between 1878 and 1879. By 1881, a one-room schoolhouse was erected in the mesquite thicket east of the later building that now houses the Mesa Historical Museum. A bell was purchased in 1884 and, during its time, also served as a community alarm signaling danger in the event of floods. This bell now sits atop the pioneer monument located on the Lehi Ward chapel grounds across the street from the Mesa Historical Museum.

In Mesa, pioneers constructed a regular schoolhouse in 1882. Books were scarce, so Bibles and copies of the Book of Mormon were utilized for reading, with spelling matches held every Friday. One early teacher recalled that even grown men and women attended class when time permitted, further evidencing the commitment to education of early residents.

Another school established during this time was a church day school for the Pima and Maricopa children living on the north side of the Salt River. Beginning in 1884, local teachers from Lehi and Mesa taught Native American students reading, arithmetic, writing, and music. The Bureau of Indian Affairs eventually assumed responsibility for this school.

In 1970, Earl Merrill, a teacher himself, summed up these early attempts at educating the children of Lehi and Mesa. "The buildings were makeshift—tents, brush sheds, or lean-tos. The teachers, though dedicated, had had no professional training. The furniture was boxes at first, and later, hand-made tables and benches. Books were scarce, and most teaching supplies considered essential today were non-existent. It was considered a great educational advancement when a home-made blackboard and 'real' chalk were introduced."

Original Lehi and Mesa schoolhouses were constructed of sun-dried adobes. Later a decorative veneer of Lehi brick and several rooms were added to the Lehi school (above in 1902). At the west entrance hung a bell, which was moved in 1914 to the new school (now Mesa Historical Museum). The bell was used for over 50 years, tolling at 8:30 a.m., 9:00 a.m., recess, noon, and 4:00 p.m. (Barbara Nielsen.)

This one-room adobe schoolhouse at the Mesa Historical Museum is a full-size replica of the first schoolhouse in Mesa. The original structure was built in 1882 at Center Street and Second Avenue. It also served as a place of worship and as temporary housing for displaced Lehi and reservation residents during times of flooding. The replica was constructed as a bicentennial (1976) project of the Mesa Public Schools. (James Hunt.)

Students in Mesa wanting higher education either attended the Territorial Normal School in Tempe or Brigham Young Academy at Provo, Utah. The normal school opened its doors in February 1886; out of the original 33 enrolled, 10 students were from Mesa and 6 were from Lehi. Joseph Noble wrote, "When I had finished the 7th grade in Lehi school, the Jones boys talked me into going to the Tempe Normal school with them. . . . While at the Normal I played tennis, football, and track and became a sergeant in the Cadet Company [right]. I needed one more year to graduate but received a call to go on a mission to New Zealand and left August 1904." Below is the 1923 graduating class from the normal school. (Right Kenneth Noble; below Barbara Nielsen.)

In addition to Christmas, Easter, and Halloween, early schools in the Mesa area also celebrated May Day. The girls dressed in white above were photographed on May 1, 1891. In Lehi (below, 1929), the annual *Return of Spring* pageant became an event that involved the entire community. Held outside on the northwest corner of the school grounds, this activity included costumes and an orchestra (left). May Day was also celebrated by church groups. In 1922, the *Relief Society Magazine* reported, "During the noon recess [of a stake Relief Society conference,] a May festival was held and Mrs. [Mamie] Clark was crowned the Queen of the May," honoring her work as Stake Relief Society president. (Above Lucille Kempton; below Alice and Pat Boyle.)

Sometimes May Day would start with a big parade ending at the corner of Center Street and Second Avenue. After a picnic, there were games for the children and a baseball game. The day was finished with a dance in the evening. This photograph captures a 1949 braiding of the maypoles at the Franklin School. After World War II, May Day was discontinued because of a commonly held view that it was a Communist holiday. (Mesa Historical Museum.)

This photograph of an unidentified archer, labeled "Return of Prosperius," may be from an adaptation of Shakespeare's play *The Tempest*, where Prospero, the deposed Duke of Milan, is exiled on an island with his daughter Miranda. The spirit Aerial and servant Caliban help negotiate Prospero's return to Naples. Many Mesa teachers taught from the classics, including Shakespeare. (Mesa Historical Museum.)

The first high school classes in Mesa were held in 1899. Because the district owned no buses, students rode horses, drove buggies, pedaled bicycles, or walked. By 1909, a new building was completed. It featured a cafeteria and a swimming pool in the basement. The pool did not last long as the new building soon needed extra classrooms. Later a gym and auditorium were added. (ASU Library CP.LA.237.S6X.)

Lee Huber rode this bus in 1938 as a first grader. He said, "The seats were two long wooden benches on either side of the bus. The girls occupied one side and the boys the other. . . . In cold weather, canvas flaps were lowered and buckled down over the open side areas. A long pipe ran down the center of the bus, and the exhaust fumes in the pipe served as our heater." (Mesa Historical Museum.)

In the fall of 1946, Mesa High School purchased a new bus, specifically for use by auxiliaries and athletic teams. Above is the first football team to enter the bus. The photograph at right was labeled, "Shirley Merrill dedicates the Jackrabbit bus." It was reported that the bus was christened using a bottle of carrot juice. Immediately after, the football team took its first ride, whereupon one of the team remarked it was like "riding on a cloud." (Both Mesa Historical Museum.)

Harvey L. Taylor, Superintendent
M. H. S. 1933-52

Harvey L. Taylor was superintendent of Mesa Public Schools from 1933 to 1953. During his administration, he oversaw the construction of Mesa Junior High School, the first of its kind in Arizona. Taylor believed junior high–age children were less understood and more neglected than any other group. Too old for elementary and too young for senior high school, they were left stranded in the middle. (Mesa Historical Museum.)

Many prominent Latter-day Saints have given generously of their time and talents by serving on the school board. Using WPA (Works Progress Administration) and PWA (Public Works Administration) grants, an auditorium and classrooms were added to the high school in 1937. Going over blueprints for the additions are, from left to right, Harvey Taylor, Alma Davis, Wayne Denson, Arnold Huber, Frank Pomeroy, and Cecil Drew. Grateful students dedicated their 1937 yearbook to these men. (Mesa Historical Museum.)

James Brookbank (right) portrays the Aztec emperor Montezuma in the fourth *Pageant of the Superstitions* (first pageant May 1934). Held at an outdoor theater located at Double Knolls (also known as Twin Buttes) east of Mesa, it featured a cast and band of several hundred Mesa High students. It was written by Bertha Kleinman (below with son Dan in 1938) and directed by Harvey Taylor; the band was conducted by Walter Bond. Velma Davis remembered being "lucky enough to be one of the dancers" in 1938. "I wore an Indian costume and I loved it. I never minded the practices, the heat, or the snakes. . . . When the last light faded into the desert darkness, another magnificent production had been added to the fame of Mesa High School, but the important thing for most of us was the friends we made." (Right Mesa Public Library; below photograph by Max Hunt.)

About 1908, Mary Holladay from Pima taught this vocal class (above) in Mesa. Her students included, from left to right, (first row) Winnie LeBaron, Ada Standage, Leona Passey, Louise Blackburn, and Irene Noble; (second row) Leo Hibbert, Lottie Noble, teacher Mary Holladay, Mabel Pomeroy, Rose Babbitt, and Jess Stewart; (third row) George Macdonald, Frank Ellsworth, Elmer Johnson, Artimus Millett, Leonard Dykes, and Joseph Noble. About this time, Joseph Noble was also managing the dances in the Mesa (Vance/Mezona) Opera House, where Maude Sirrine was playing in the orchestra. He said, "I never dreamed that there was any chance for me with her, until I asked to take her home one night. She readily consented and that was it." Below is the orchestra at Mesa High School with their instruments, no date. (Above Kenneth Noble; below Mesa Historical Museum.)

Orchestra

The Mesa High School marching band in their new uniforms led a "Rally Parade," shown here passing the Valley National Bank, as part of the activities for the 1938 M-Men and Gleaner Conference. The newspaper reported, "Mesa streets and business houses will be decorated in green and gold, Mutual Improvement association colors, in recognition of the convention." (Photograph by Max Hunt.)

Under the direction of Linwood Noble, the Mesa High School band also played for the dedication of the Whitlow Ranch Dam on Queen Creek near Florence Junction on October 1, 1960. This earthen-filled dam was 130 feet high and part of the Roosevelt Water Conservation District. Hostesses were students from Chandler High School. (Photograph by Milo F. Ryan, ASU Arizona Collection, CP.CTH.980.)

Latter-day Saints enjoyed participating in a wide variety of activities and clubs during high school. Above is the 1922–1923 girls' basketball team in uniform; note their footgear. Below at an unknown date is the Sub Deb Smoothies Club sponsored by Esther Calloway (back row center). There were at least 13 LDS girls in this club. The year 1948 proved eventful as school administrators discontinued the school's scheduled activity period, and clubs were then required to meet before school, during lunch, or after school. This affected 24 associations, including four honor clubs. (Above Barbara Nielsen; below Lila Booth.)

One well-loved organization from Mesa High was the Rabbettes. Originally organized in 1925 as a pep-club called El Connettes, they were reorganized in 1931 by Bobby Petrie and renamed Peppettes. When they changed to the Rabbettes, Marjorie Entz became their sponsor. Entz remembered a membership of 113: "It got out of hand—it was crazy but a lot of fun." During World War II when shoes were rationed, the girls "had to construct fake boots out of white oilcloth. The girls hated them because they fell off a lot," Entz said. "Every band has flags and rifles, but back then hardly anyone had flags, and no one had ropers except Mesa High." Above is the 1949 New Year's Day Salad Bowl parade; below are, from left to right, Nita Bradshaw, Nola Elder, Lavonne Gilbert, Leona Coates, and Marvel Nichols with Dean Larsen. (Both Mesa Historical Museum.)

Rabbette and Band Leader

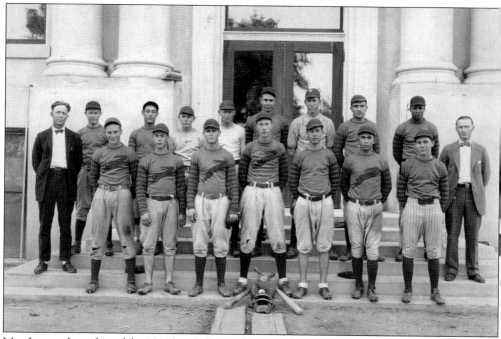

Members and coaches of the 1926 baseball team have set down books and bats for their photograph. Note Mesa High's Jackrabbit is pictured on some of the shirts. Nolan Pulliam (far right) was head coach; he also taught history and math. The yearbook reports that "the Jackrabbits won the right to compete for the State Baseball Championship with Glendale by defeating Superior by a score of 4-2." (Catherine Ellis.)

One athletic event in the Salt River Valley was donkey basketball, here in 1956. Sometimes the teams were fathers against sons, other times one group of students against another. At times, burlap was placed on the feet of the donkeys so their hoofs did not ruin the gym floor. This activity was later discontinued as inhumane. (Mesa Historical Museum.)

Many Latter-day Saint athletes have excelled within the public school system. At right, Cyrus Russell, an outstanding end player for Mesa High School, poses in his football uniform. He was a member of the 1939 All-State football team and played in the Southwest Conference championship game. (Donetta Bowers.)

Linwood Noble (left) was band director at Mesa High School for many years and donated this uniform to the Mesa Historical Museum. Ray Russell and Eva Sue Johnson (right) are the 1949 Homecoming king and queen. Russell, an exceptional athlete, was rated one of the top four hurdlers in the nation while at Kansas State University. (Both Mesa Historical Society.)

Under the guidance of Rulon Shepherd (elementary superintendent) and Harvey Taylor (high school superintendent), all schools in Mesa were consolidated in 1946 into one district. The ultimate service project (or ultimate detention) is seen in this photograph of LeRoy Peel taking the gum off the seats in the auditorium at the Mesa High School (left). Below, instructor Don C. Lillywhite is teaching a physics class using an experiment on light on April 29, 1954. The students are, from left to right, Bruce Rogers, Lillywhite, Alan Kleinman, Gerald O'Barr, and Mark Turley. (Both Mesa Historical Museum.)

Barbara Crandall taught elementary school in Chandler, Lehi, and Mesa for over 20 years, winning the respect and affection of her students. She also served as Maricopa Stake Primary president. Each year, she hosted a luau for her elementary school class with the students performing for their parents. (Barbara Nielsen.)

Sarah Cortez graduated from Mesa High School in 1949 as one of six Hispanic graduates and the only Latter-day Saint. Pictured here are, from left to right, (first row) Cortez and Juanita Perez; (second row) Ray Armenta, Frank Valenzuela, and Joe Arvayo. Not pictured is Nadine Gonzalez. (Sarah Dixon.)

Arlene Shepherd Bateman, daughter of longtime superintendent of Mesa public schools Rulon Shepherd, is one of the many accomplished Latter-day Saint women who attended Mesa High School. She participated in student government, service clubs, drama, and music and performed with the lovely girls shown above. She also was the accompanist for the Chansonettes (below), a mid-1940s teenage choral group led by Mabel Macdonald. Arlene attended Brigham Young University and in 1948 returned to Mesa to teach. (Both Arlene Bateman.)

Chansonettes, led by Mabel Macdonald about 1944 or possibly 1945. Left to right: Wilma Winterton, Marian Killian, Georgia Ellsworth, Polly Bowden, Mabel Macdonald, Wini Ellsworth, Jean Anderson, Sharlimae Clouse, Charmaine Guthrie, Hazel Dawn Macdonald, Arlene Shepherd, accompanist.

The first release-time seminary for high school students began in 1912. Classes were held at the Mesa Second Ward building, one block from the high school. The 1923 graduating class is pictured above. In September 1938, an official seminary building was completed. Today seminary buildings are located near all junior and high schools in Mesa. (Lila Booth.)

An Institute of Religion was organized in 1948 following a petition signed by approximately 120 ASU students. Dad Mann's beer garden was purchased and cleaned up for this purpose. A Lambda Delta Sigma chapter (a sorority administered by the LDS Church) was also organized. Pictured here is a *c.* 1946 meeting at the home of Eloise Randall, their advisor (and Gleaner leader). Some of the girls include Flora Bateman, Luana Brimley, Kathleen Flake, Lorna Fish, Lora Mortenson, LeOla Rogers, Ruby Rogers, Ann Shumway, Shirley Shumway, Leora Tryon, Paula Udall, and Edith Udall. (LeOla Leavitt.)

G. Homer Durham came to Arizona State University in 1960 and was president for nine years. He inherited a campus with no apparent design, a faculty of only 49 percent Ph.D.s, and a university that still mainly produced teachers. He immediately began plans for new buildings, including Grady Gammage Memorial Auditorium (Durham shown above left at the ground-breaking with Grady Gammage Jr. wielding the shovel). Durham also awarded the first Ph.D. degrees given at ASU (below, at far right, in 1963). With a special interest in the arts, Durham promoted the ASU Art Museum and often played the piano for informal gatherings. For the 1985 hymnbook, he teamed up with Gordon B. Hinckley, a former missionary companion, for the hymn "My Redeemer Lives." Durham believed democracy includes a "willingness to abide dissent and disagreement." (ASU University Archives; above UP.ASUP.F33.1168, below UP.ASUP.F331168a.)

Three

THE MARICOPA STAKE

Early schoolhouses in both Lehi and Mesa served dual functions: as places to educate children and as community centers for religious worship and social gatherings. Conversely, church buildings such as the Mesa Tabernacle and the Mezona were used for graduations and other assemblies when a large meeting space was required for educational purposes.

One example of a religious meeting held within the community schoolhouse occurred on Sunday, December 10, 1882. At this time, the largest crowd ever assembled in Mesa gathered at the adobe schoolhouse. Under the direction of elders Erastus Snow and Moses Thatcher of the Quorum of Twelve Apostles, the Maricopa Stake of Zion was organized. Today this is the oldest such ecclesiastical unit within the state still bearing its original name.

A hundred years later, there were 25 stakes within the original Maricopa Stake boundaries. The first division was in 1938 with the creation of the Phoenix Stake; then Mesa Stake was created in 1946. These three stakes worked together to build the Tri-Stake Center (later renamed the Interstake Center). Pres. Harold Wright remembered "one year going to the wards and asking everyone to set aside one Christmas and not buy any gifts for anyone over the age of 12. The money we would have spent was to go into the building fund. Everyone really responded, even the little children. . . . I think it was during that time that we dedicated three chapels in one weekend."

For the centennial celebration, Jeanne Wright and Arlene Bateman wrote the play *Our Maricopa Stake House*. Using vignettes and musical numbers, this production recounted how Mesa and Lehi were settled and honored each of the stake presidents by portraying their accomplishments. A cast of over 100 stake members presented the production twice to packed houses. In a history of the Maricopa Stake, Wanda LeBaron wrote, "Much could be written . . . of great leaders and members, both men and women. As the writer, I could name hundreds myself, but it could not be done and do justice to all. Please know that the unnamed are as great and precious as the named."

In 1927, James McClintock published this photograph of the first five Maricopa Stake presidents: (1) Alexander MacDonald, (2) Charles Robson, (3) Collins Hakes, (4) John LeSueur, and (5) James LeSueur. The Maricopa Stake was organized in 1880 with MacDonald as president; in 1887, he moved to Chihuahua, Mexico, to help pioneer there. Robson then served until 1894. During Hakes's presidency, membership in the stake was as follows: Papago Ward, 1,219; Mesa Ward, 648; Lehi Ward, 200; Alma Ward, 282; and Nephi Ward, 104. (The Papago Ward included all Native American converts in southern Arizona.) In 1905, Hakes moved to Bluewater, New Mexico, and John LeSueur was asked to move from St. Johns to Mesa to preside over the stake (which he did until 1912). Upon LeSueur's release, his son, James, became president. James wrote, "I was stunned and insisted that I was but a boy. . . . I was 33 years old." (Church Archives P2913-6.)

Past presidents of the Maricopa Stake include two sets of fathers and sons: John and James LeSueur and Lorenzo "Lo" and Harold Wright. Pictured above from left to right are Lo Wright, James R. Price, James W. LeSueur, and John T. LeSueur. During James LeSueur's presidency (1912–1924), the stake had 22 construction projects, including remodeling the Mezona and building 14 chapels, two mission homes, one swimming pool, and the temple. LeSueur, estimating that the projects totaled $1,075,000, wrote, "This may be a record of any Stake during the same period of time. We had the name of always asking for money for construction." Harold Wright (right) served from 1948 to 1970, and two large donations of land, one in Queen Creek and the other along the Chandler Highway, greatly enlarged the stake farm. (Both Jeanne Wright.)

Construction began on a Mesa tabernacle in 1895. It was dedicated in December 1896 by Brigham Young Jr. of the Twelve Apostles. Earl Merrill wrote, "The building, with its high, vaulted interior, balcony, and chandeliers, was used for stake conferences and other gatherings, such as high school graduations, until about 1919, when the Church acquired the Vance Auditorium (later, the Mezona) and began holding its large assemblages there." (Mesa Historical Museum.)

Adults of the Mesa First Ward are shown here in front of their meetinghouse in 1910. Another photograph shows the Sunday School children. When the Maricopa Stake was first organized in 1882, it consisted of the Jonesville (Lehi) and Mesa Wards and Tempe Branch. It was not until 1912 that Mesa Second Ward was formed. (Lucille Kempton.)

Latter-day Saint families living in Gilbert at the dawn of the 20th century were part of the Chandler Ward. Members chopped maize to raise funds to purchase a piano. An early Chandler Sunday School is shown above. Below, Gilbert had its own Sunday School by 1923. Sunday Schools taught both gospel principles and church hymns, particularly to children. Hymns such as "Welcome, Welcome Sabbath Morning" and "Thanks for the Sabbath School" were favorites, but No. 79 reminded everyone of the time: "Never be late to the Sunday School class, Come with your bright sunny faces; . . . Try to be there, always be there, Promptly at ten in the morning." (Both Barbara Nielsen.)

In the early 1930s, when someone spoke of Bishop Dana, they may have meant Isaac Dana, bishop of Mesa First Ward; his brother Hugh Dana, bishop of Mesa Third Ward; or their cousin, Clarence Dana, bishop of Mesa Second Ward. This photograph of Bishop Hugh Dana (center) was taken in June 1933, twenty miles northeast of Mesa on an Aaronic Priesthood annual outing. (Utah State Historical Society C2.3-20.)

In the 1930s and 1940s, the older Primary boys were Trail Builders (with the tree symbol at the bottom of their bandelos); 9-year-olds were Blazers, 10-year-olds were Trekkers, and 11-year-olds were Guides. Pictured above is Monty Dana (second row, far left) about 1938 in a group that may include boys ages 9–11. (Nancy Norton.)

In the 1950s, the Young Women's Mutual Improvement Association (YWMIA) included classes for girls 12–13 years old (Beehives), 14–15 (Mia Maids), 16–18 (Junior Gleaners, later changed to Laurels), and 19–20 (Gleaners). This is a Gleaner class in the 1950s. As Wanda LeBaron wrote, "Many outstanding programs came under the auspices of the Mutual through the years. Many talents were developed, many leaders trained, and many testimonies built." (Barbara Nielsen.)

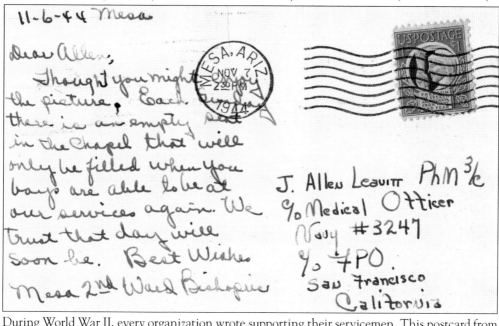

During World War II, every organization wrote supporting their servicemen. This postcard from the Mesa Second Ward Bishopric, noting a missing place in the congregation, had a photograph of their chapel and went to Joseph Allen Leavitt, later a prominent obstetrician in Mesa. During his enlistment, Leavitt served as a pharmacist mate on the island of Tinian in the Mariana Islands. (Barbara Lanier.)

Born in 1905 in Chuichupa, Mexico, longtime Mesa resident Fred Johnson moved to the Salt River Valley in 1927. A talented contractor, he became noted for his work on LDS buildings, including the Tri-Stake Center, Bishops' Storehouse, and various chapels. In 1964, he was called on a work mission to build a chapel in Santiago, Chile, where he taught the art of brick making to other missionaries along with the gospel. (Fred Johnson Jr.)

With three stakes (Maricopa, Phoenix, and Mesa) in the Salt River Valley, ground was broken for a huge Tri-Stake Center in 1953. Pictured above in November 1954 when under construction, it was completed in 1957. The building provided housing for temple excursions from Mexico and Central America and was used for conferences, athletics, fairs, banquets, and dances. The name was later changed to Interstake Center. (Church Archives P5505-16.)

The welfare program of the LDS Church was born during the Depression. Wanda LeBaron wrote that in 1936, when a Bishops' Storehouse was established, "The Relief Societies were asked to remodel clothing, make quilts, etc. The clothing was to be conditioned so that anyone would be proud to wear them." This has been one goal of the used clothing store, Deseret Industries, which was established in 1963. (Mesa Historical Museum.)

Early Mormon settlers were farmers producing citrus, cotton, and alfalfa. This farming experience (and equipment) helped when Queen Creek Ward needed to raise $40,000 as their assessment for a new chapel. A gigantic cotton picking day was organized, with about 15 mechanical pickers donated by ward members and neighbors. In one day, the ward raised $4,500 for their new building. (Stan Turley.)

In 1921, the Papago Indian Branch used the reservation school for a bazaar and sold "sandwiches, molasses cake, and soft drinks colored with berries." They cleared over $80 and donated $40 toward the Arizona temple. Relief Society president was Nellie Santeo. The above 1949 photograph was taken at the dedication of their Relief Society building with Santeo and councilors seated in front. Joseph Fielding Smith dedicated the building. Below is the adobe home of Verner Smith, bishop of the Papago Ward in 1958–1959. He was the second Pima bishop of the Papago Ward (Johnson Enos was the first). (Church Archives; above P3177-3-7, below P3177-4-2.)

This photograph is of the Phoenix First Ward Sunday School on Easter Sunday, 1944, in front of the Monroe School. The chapel for Phoenix First Ward, originally part of the Maricopa Stake but at this time part of the Phoenix Stake, was across the road from the school at Seventh and Monroe Streets. The chapel was too close to the street for a good photograph. (Church Archives P1203-1-7.)

With the Maricopa, Mesa, and Phoenix Stakes supervising wards and branches distant from their centers, some enterprising leaders traveled by small plane. In 1949, Stake Relief Society members visited branches in Ray and Hayden by "chartering" Dave Lamoreaux's airplane (as reported in the *Relief Society Magazine*). This later Stake Relief Society presidency is visiting Pine. From left to right are, Joe Farnsworth, Vida Brinton, Esther Miller, Donna Brinton, Pearl Brinton, and ? Tayrien (pilot). (Donna LeBaron.)

The Relief Society promoted culture, including these 1957 East Mesa Stake Singing Mothers in traditional white blouses, dark skirts, and a (red?) flower. They also provided relief as Mary Clark, Stake Relief Society president, described in 1927. Fifty-five Oklahomans, coming to work in the cotton fields, were without provisions. Soon "dishes, clothing and bedding, food, money, and everything necessary" filled two trucks, making it possible for the children to attend Sunday School and public schools. (Lori Lawlor.)

Relief Society women peeling apples for canning illustrate the 1936 directive from Salt Lake to can all food possible and establish a Bishops' Storehouse (located originally in an upper room of the Mezona). Clara B. Emmett served for 36 years, making the program run smoothly. Other facilities, including a modern cannery, were added, and in 1982, the multiple-unit Area Welfare Center, with 100-foot grain silos, opened to care for the poor and, more recently, relief for disasters. (Nancy Norton.)

Vida and Van Brinton and unidentified helper (right) are preparing dinner in the Mezona basement for visiting general authorities. Three generations of Brintons managed the Mezona, sometimes as a ward calling, until 1941: Van Sr., Dilworth, and Dilworth Jr. "Dad often said," wrote Dilworth Jr., "that the Mezona was the only place where you could start out as a hat checker for a dollar a night and through hard work become the manager for free." Below, Gordon B. Hinckley (left) and Pres. Spencer W. Kimball visit with Vida Brinton. Vida was Arizona's Woman of the Year in 1966. When Dilworth was being interviewed by George Albert Smith for a mission, "Most of the interview," wrote his son Dilworth Jr., "consisted of Brother Smith telling him about what a wonderful woman [his mother] Vida Brinton was." (Both Donna LeBaron.)

This photograph was labeled "A group of pioneers of Mesa, Arizona, September 1941," and includes (from left to right) Faie Newell Donaldson, Ina Pomeroy Brewer, Dora Morris Pomeroy, Frank T. Pomeroy, Warren Leroy Sirrine (oldest living pioneer of Mesa), Addie Sirrine Johnson, and Adah Crismon Byers. Frank Pomeroy began publishing the *Genealogical and Historical Magazine of the Arizona Temple District* in 1924, and the size of his personally researched pedigree chart was legendary. In 1932, he wrote about a 12-step YMMIA Book of Remembrance project: "Many of the books prepared by the youngsters are remarkable. . . . [They] have demonstrated what persistence in the work can accomplish." Below are all the people in the Mesa Fifth Ward who completed a Book of Remembrance in 1955 when John R. Allen was bishop. (Above Arizona Historical Society/Tucson 42858; below Nancy Norton.)

Delbert L. Stapley, the second son of O. S. Stapley, began working in the Mesa store as a teenager. He served in the Southern States Mission, was in the Marine Corps during World War I, and later was an officer in the Arizona National Guard. He was a member of the Phoenix Stake presidency for 13 years and in 1950 was called to the Quorum of Twelve Apostles. In 1956, he was asked to address students at Brigham Young University using his experience with the O. S. Stapley Company to cover the topic "Fundamentals for a Successful Career in Business." His eight principles for success included good buying, fair but good profit margins, proper turnover of merchandise, vigorous and constant sales planning, good accounting, efficient credit and collections, adequate operating costs control, and good employee relationships. (Both ASU Library, Herb and Dorothy McLaughlin Collection.)

Boy Scout troops are always dependent upon adult volunteers. In Lehi, Rollin Jones (also principal of the school) was the first scoutmaster, with Roy Sirrine as assistant. About 1919, the noonday meal, surreptitiously prepared for their parents, gave rise to the local place name, Coon's Bluff. The required merit badges for Eagle Scout rank help achieve the Scouting goal of preparing boys for adulthood. Above is a 1957 Eagle Court of Honor for Troop 155; pictured from left to right are Roy Powell (scoutmaster), Gary Perkins, Dewayne Cooley, Stephen Phelps, Norman McKee, and Glen Guthrie (assistant scoutmaster). Cooley and Phelps are Explorer scouts. The photograph at left was the front page of the February 12, 1984, *Church News*. Pictured are three generations of Eagle Scouts, Wayne (seated left), Stephen, and Kent (standing) Phelps. (Both Stephen Phelps.)

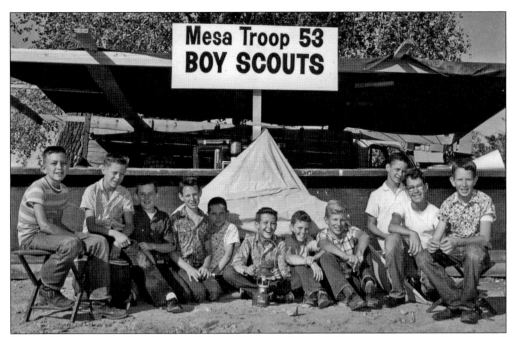

Pictured here are the Boy Scouts of Troop 53 around one of their tents after an all-night vigil guarding the equipment and props necessary for the dedication ceremonies of Whitlow Ranch Dam, held October 1, 1960. Dale Cooper was scoutmaster and Al Jennings assistant scoutmaster. (Photograph by Milo F. Ryan, Arizona Collection, ASU CP.CTH.983.)

In 1982, Maricopa Stake president Dea Montague organized a massive Boy Scout Jamboree called "High on the Mountain Top." With over 7,000 Scouts attending from around the state, it reportedly took 120 priests and 250 deacons 23 minutes to administer and pass the Sacrament. Visiting general authorities included Hartman Rector Jr., H. Burke Peterson, Rex D. Pinegar, and Vaughn J. Featherstone. (Jay Tenney.)

"High on the Mountain Top," the classic Latter-day Saint missionary hymn, is based on Isaiah 2: 2–3. With this theme and choosing a location in Arizona's high, ponderosa pine–covered mountains, a spectacular jamboree was held. Using the opening words of the hymn, "High on the mountain top a banner is unfurled," these Scouts (above) have created and display their own banners. The weeklong camp included Scouting activities, missionary preparation, hiking, camping, a laser light show, and a service project. Under supervision of the U.S. Forest Service, the Scouts planted 21,000 ponderosa pine seedlings. Ty Beavers is shown at left working on this project. The project saved the forest service more than $12,000 in planting costs. (Both Jay Tenney.)

A descendant and namesake of Capt. Jefferson Hunt of the Mormon Battalion, Jeff Hunt (right) decided in 2000 to do an Eagle project for Mesa's Mormon Battalion reenactors. Their replica wagon needed refurbishing, and the first step was to rehydrate the wood. A uniquely Mesa solution seemed obvious: lower the wagon into an empty swimming pool and fill the pool with water (below). The wagon was also repaired and painted. Many area Scouts earn the Mormon Battalion patch by hiking 15 miles of the trail and learning the history, often with a campfire program by the reenactors. Mesa District always has a large number of Eagle Scouts. In 2007, a total of 342 boys earned their Eagle rank with 56,372 service hours. (Both James Hunt.)

Initially, young women from Mesa and Lehi spent summer recreation time in the Pinal Mountains near Globe. Then in 1938, Pres. Lo Wright arranged the purchase of 155 acres near Pine. Amenities included hiking trails, a barn, and a bowery nicknamed "The Sacred Grove." The camp was christened LoMIA in honor of Wright, and the cost for a week was $5, including transportation. On Sundays, the girls walked a mile to Pine for church. Today Camp LoMIA consists of three separate camps with over 40 cabins, three covered dining areas, and a lodge. Above, girls from the Mesa 11th Ward attended camp in 1961 and posed in front of one of the cabins. Below, Vanessa Martinez is looking over music to be sung at the 2007 camp. (Above Nancy Norton; below Jennifer Turner.)

Today many youth groups enjoy learning about their Mormon heritage by reliving a small part of the early pioneer experience through elaborate reenactments. Usually handcarts are used and participants dress in pioneer costumes (above is a Lehi group in the White Mountains). Pioneer stories are told at points along the way, and often a 10-pound sack of flour "baby" dies and is buried. The trek is usually 15 miles, a significant distance for most adults and youth, and leaders dressed as angels (below) sometimes help push the handcarts over particularly difficult spots. (Both Duane Burt.)

Pablo Cortez came to the United States at age 17 from Jalisco, Mexico, about 1900. He moved to Arizona, where he met and married Mercedes Jaramillo in 1918. While in Mesa, their sons began playing basketball with the Spanish branch. Their daughter Sarah recalled only one branch and that the missionaries were living in the branch building. Other prominent families during the early years of the Spanish branch were Alejandro and Josepha Arredondo, Don and Cleotilda Gutierrez, Guillermo Lopez, Mercedes and Pedro Martinez, Juan Pagan, and Juan Romero. Today there are over a dozen Spanish-speaking congregations in the area (and one Tongan ward). Below, sister missionaries Jackie Elmore (left) and Mindy Anderson attend the 1995 Liahona Second Ward baptism of Santos Avalos (center left) and Jesus Anaya (center right) with member David Fernandez (left) and ward mission leader David Garcia (right). (Above Sarah Dixon; below Jackie Ellis.)

Adalberto Partida is pictured here dressed as a Mexican *charro* in an authentic costume he made himself. Originally from Sinaloa, he and his family enjoy performing traditional dances for both church and community events. Partida, a member of the Adobe Branch, Apache Junction Stake, is preparing to dance the *jarabe tapatio*, a traditional dance from Jalisco, at the Gilbert Stake Center in 2004. (Laura Partida.)

Keith Teller (at left with wife Linda) participated in the Indian Placement Program in Mesa during the 1970s. This program began after World War II and averaged, at peak, 2,500 students living in LDS homes during the academic year. While in Mesa, Teller attended Mesa 13th Ward and was on the Westwood High School football team. (Barbara Nielsen.)

Pictured above is the Arizona Mormon Choir at the Assembly Hall in Salt Lake City. Organized during the LDS Church's sesquicentennial celebration as the Central Arizona Mormon Choir, the group has undergone several name changes and is today known as the Deseret Chorale. The choir has produced several CDs and has performed at Grady Gammage Auditorium in Tempe, at St. George, Utah, and at the Salt Lake Tabernacle (below) with the Mormon Tabernacle Choir. (Above Jaynie Payne; below John and Linda Berry.)

Four

A HERITAGE OF CULTURE

Early leaders such as Joseph Smith Jr. and Brigham Young promoted the power of positive play, extolling the virtues of wholesome recreation and cultural pursuits as well as civic and social interactions. Promoting his personal motto of eight hours work, eight hours sleep, and eight hours recreation daily, Brigham Young encouraged programs of dance, music, and drama.

Despite poverty, early Latter-day Saints in the Salt River Valley continued to promote recreational activities, including dances, orations, and plays. Lehi settlers recorded that, during their first summer, moonlight swimming parties or watermelon feasts were held frequently, in spite of (or because of) the extreme heat. Community socials were held both at the old fort in Lehi and the Pomeroy bowery in Mesa. Dirt floors were packed hard to facilitate dancing.

This distinctive cultural feature of Mesa Latter-day Saints continued to develop over the next century. Church events often overlapped with municipal affairs, including pageants, parades, picnics, and displays. The Boy Scouts of America program was adopted and elaborate camps for girls were constructed, both part of the Mutual Improvement Association. Gymnasiums and ball fields appeared with increasing frequency at new meetinghouses, allowing for interchurch athletic leagues. Public parks and playgrounds were constructed, and the Vance Auditorium was purchased, remodeled, and renamed the Mezona. It functioned as an amusement hall with public dances, picture shows, and roller-skating and also served as a town meeting hall for high school graduations and other public gatherings.

Today groups with a specific LDS interest are common, including Daughters of Utah Pioneers, the Mormon Battalion Association, Sons of Utah Pioneers, and the Deseret Chorale, formerly known as both the Central Arizona and the Arizona Mormon Choir. The most important church-sponsored public events, however, are the annual Easter Pageant and the Christmas light display, both on the temple grounds. These are open to the public as a gift to the community.

Early recreation, particularly when visitors came from out of town, sometimes included trips to the Casa Grande ruins 40 miles south of Mesa. Nearby are the remnants of a 17-mile canal that reaches the Gila River. Today the ruins are a national monument. It is believed the protective roof over the ruins was built in 1932 by Albert Coplan, a Mesa contractor. (Kenneth Bond.)

Outings into the desert were common, as seen in this c. 1912 LeSueur photograph. From left to right are Merle Skousen, Eunice Shurtliff, Leo LeSueur, Charles LeSueur (driver), Jean Hunsaker, Leola LeSueur, and Karl LeSueur. Red Mountain is seen in the background with a lone saguaro, sometimes called an Arizona cucumber by the pioneers. (Mesa Historical Museum.)

Community and ward campouts, then as now, were planned regularly. One of the earliest was in 1895, with nearly the entire town participating, including a choir and a brass band. "Sleepouts," sometimes in the dry riverbed, featured campfire programs and star gazing. Some campers recalled that on clear nights one could see all the way to the Tempe Bridge. Above is a Lehi Ward picnic east of Mesa about 1920. Below, the ward members have stretched a volleyball net between two cars. (Both Glynna Reinsch.)

Mesa residents have participated in the LDS Church's massive intramural sports programs through the years. Winners frequently traveled to Salt Lake City to participate in championship tournaments. The 1924 Yellow Jackets church basketball team from Gilbert included, from left to right, (first row) Myron Crandall, Paul Crandall, Edwin Miller, Wilford Phelps, and Merrill Hatch; (second row) Orwell Vance, Loren Allen, Joe B. Maier (coach), and George Freestone. (Barbara Nielsen.)

John Seymour Allen (right) moved to Mesa in 1881 at age 11. Allen was proud of his large family of 12 children, which included these seven sons. While living in Gilbert, in 1934, he organized and coached the Allen family basketball team and challenged any family in the church to a game. Team members are, from left to right, Joseph, Loren, Gove, John R., Ashael, Russell, and Ben. (Barbara Nielsen.)

In central Arizona, it is usually possible to hold Thanksgiving dinner outside. This *c.* 1931 Bond family dinner was held at Bond Corner (University and Country Club Drives). Grandparents are Prudence Pricilla and Joseph W. Bond (seated in foreground). Standing are John and Pearl Horne, who owned a dairy on today's Horne Road. (Kenneth Bond.)

In 1945, Owen Stradling took an interest in flying. By April 1946, he had his pilot's license and leased land on North Mesa Boulevard (now Country Club Drive). There he built the first airport in Mesa, alternately called Stradling's Airfield, Mesa Airport, and Hopkins Stradling Air Field. He offered all aircraft-related services. He even scheduled days when one could fly over and see Mesa for $1. (Phillip Stradling.)

Pioneer Day celebrates Mormon pioneers first entering the Salt Lake Valley on July 24, 1847. Observed as early as 1849 in Utah, this day usually included music, barbecues, rodeos, parades, sporting events, and pageants. This square dance may not be for Pioneer Day, but Hugh Dana (right, in suit) and his wife, Helen (left, in dark dress), lead this Mesa Third Ward activity. (Nancy Norton.)

Barbara Phelps (later Allen) arrived in Mesa in 1879 as a 16-month-old infant. At age 12, she received an accordion for Christmas. She then earned money by playing with her father, Hyrum Phelps, for dances in Lehi, especially at Christmas. In later life, she organized the Granny Band, which performed at events around town. From left to right are Deborah Nelson, Julia Watkins, unidentified, Barbara Allen, unidentified, Lora Hancock, and Lizzie Rust. (Barbara Nielsen.)

The first camp of the Daughters of Utah Pioneers (DUP) was organized in Mesa in 1924. DUP members have been active in collecting history and artifacts and in raising funds for monuments and preservation of materials. This 1946 meeting of the Anna K. Kleinman Camp and Ox Bow Camp (from Tempe) honored Cassie Pomeroy (seated center) as the first DUP president in Mesa. (Mesa Historical Museum.)

Stories of the early history of the *Akimel Au-Authm* (Pimas) and *Xalychidom* (Maricopas) were passed down on long winter nights and also told in dance. A Pima, Dorothy Lewis, said, "The dances are half religious and half legends." The participants in this 1960s dance group, led by Leonard Carlos (back left) and Claudina Wood (front left, granddaughter of Incarnacion Valenzuela), were mostly Latter-day Saints. (Church Archives, P4451.4.)

On February 14, 1908, entrepreneur John Vance opened an auditorium that would influence the lives of Mesa and Salt River Valley residents for many years. Featuring a hard maple floor for dancing, the 130-by-100-foot barn-like structure at various times featured roller-skating, theater, concerts, motion pictures, and prominent speakers. Its regularly scheduled Friday night dances became legendary as a spot where young love first blossomed. In 1919, the church purchased the building and began using it for stake offices, a Bishop's Storehouse, and place of worship. The *New Pioneers on the March* pageant (above) was presented in 1941 at a quarterly stake conference. At left, Helen Crismon (left) and Arlene Bateman decorate (in January 1963) for one of the many Gold and Green Balls held at the Mezona. (Above Jeanne Wright; left Mesa Historical Museum.)

A popular act around town was the Wrights' spoof of Disneyland's Golden Horseshoe Revue. For their act, Jeanne Wright was Sluefoot Sue, Jack Wright (center) was Pecos Bill and Wally Boag, and Tom Wright was The Golden Tenor. The Wright family's trips (including friends) to Disneyland were legendary. (Jeanne Wright.)

Many LDS women have contributed greatly to the Mesa community. Jeanne Wright and Arlene Bateman were co–Mesa Women of the Year for 1980. Wright helped establish the Christmas lights display at the temple, helped organize "Horizons '83" (a mega 61-stake Young Women's conference), founded Teen Elect to teach social graces, and opened a chain of dance studios in 1959. (Jeanne Wright.)

Mesa city fathers planned and set aside land for community parks. One such park was the Rendezvous. A skating rink, baseball diamonds, basketball courts, and picnic areas made this particular park a popular spot for family reunions (such as the one pictured above with the Richins family) and church activities (like the girls' summer Primary pictured below). Later a swimming pool, complete with a brick bathhouse, chlorination system, and free Red Cross swimming lessons, was opened. Water from the pool was used for irrigation. Other parks to be associated with Latter-day Saints are Pioneer, Kleinman, Reed, Stapley, and Park of the Canals. (Above Kenneth Bond; below Donna LeBaron.)

The city of Mesa celebrated its Diamond Jubilee by presenting a spectacular pageant May 7–8, 1953. Bertha Kleinman wrote the script, Rulon Shepherd directed it, and local artists painted the scenery (above). Presented on a football field, real horses and wagons were used to tell the history of this area from Native Americans to Spanish explorers to Mormon Battalion soldiers to Mormon settlers to the present (below). (Both Mesa Historical Museum.)

One hallmark event associated with early Mesa that continued sporadically into the 1990s was the Mesa Day Miniature Parade. Begun in 1936 in connection with the citrus fair, Boy Scouts pulled as many as 150 pint-sized floats through downtown Mesa. David Johnson recalled that on one occasion, the handle on his family's entry (Watson's Flower Shop) broke and inventive Scouts pulled the wagon with their belts. (Nancy Norton.)

Thalia Kartchner, originally from Snowflake, was a teacher loved by many Mesa children. She taught fourth grade at Alma School, and this Miniature Parade float from her class was pulled by, from left to right, Frank Piña, Ned Reed, Kenneth Bond, and Manuel Ocamora. In later life, she received a plaque honoring her for teaching school when Arizona achieved statehood in 1912. (Dilworth Brinton Jr.)

Irene Watson raised flowers in her yard and began selling small bouquets for 25¢ to people visiting sick friends at a nearby hospital. In 1927, this became the basis for a thriving flower shop. Above are two photographs of her daughter, Eva, who served as head surgical nurse at Mesa Southside Hospital in addition to working at the shop. From its inception, Watson's Flower Shop made it a family tradition to build floats from flowers for parades in Mesa. Pictured at right is a Miniature Parade entry for 1997 with Angela Quist (left) and Leah Burk. Although the parade has been discontinued by the city, Watson's continues this tradition in surrounding communities. (All David Johnson.)

In 1946, the Mesa Junior Chamber of Commerce (Jaycees) began organizing an annual Rawhide Roundup, turning Main Street into an Old West town complete with rides and entertainment. Continuing into the 1960s, this event included many fund-raising activities, among which was the practice of "arresting" citizens who then made pledges to secure their release from jail. At left, Innes Robson (left) and Wayne Peterson are being arrested by officers Lee Moore and Joe True (right). Below, Bobby Leavitt and Bob Goodman "languish" in the city jail. In 1950, local dentist Wayne Peterson served as president of the Mesa Jaycees. (Left Lee Peterson; below Barbara Lanier.)

Dance festivals, many of which were spectacular both with dances and costumes, have been popular youth activities used to promote culture and friendship. Pictured here is a 2006 tri-stake dance festival entitled *Light Up the World*. With approximately 800 performers, organizers prepared over a year for the event that featured professional scenery and special effects, including an appearance by paragliders. Pictured above are, from left to right, David Solheim, Tunufa'l Ta'ase, Alex Arnold, Josh Roberts, and Joseph Turner. Ta'ase is the drummer for Kilali's Polynesian Review. He and Laupanana I'aulualo (caller and drummer) taught the young men a Samoan dance (below). On November 18, around 4,000 spectators attended the two performances given that night. (Both Danette Turner.)

A series of M-Men and Gleaner conferences began in 1935, with Snowflake providing a barbecue breakfast and dancing under the stars. Later conferences were held in Safford (1936 with a breakfast dance) and Tucson (1937 with the dedication of a Mormon Battalion monument). In 1938, the conference was held in Mesa (left); presidents Marzelle Jesperson and Ed Noble planned the program. (Photograph by Max Hunt.)

This entry for the M-Men and Gleaner parade illustrates the unspoken purpose of the conference: meeting a potential husband or wife. A tractor pulls a flatbed trailer with a bride and groom (plus small children) and the signs, "Matrimonial Agency" and "Result of Recreation." (Photograph by Max Hunt.)

Also for the parade, Gleaner Girls from El Paso, Texas, decorated their car with "Headquarters Mezona." The Mezona with its dance floor became the meeting place for many couples. Keith W. Perkins wrote that, not only his parents, but he and his wife, Vella, "met for the first time" there and "courted on the dance floor of the old Mezona hall." (Photograph by Max Hunt.)

Probably the most important part of this conference, however, was the Easter sunrise service on April 17 (above). It began at 5:30 a.m. on the grounds next to the temple. The program included congregational and special musical numbers with speakers Harvey Taylor and Ridge Hicks. (Photograph by Max Hunt.)

Today the Easter pageant is billed as the "World's Largest Annual Outdoor Easter Pageant." It has evolved from a simple sunrise service at Tempe Butte in 1928 to a sunrise service on the steps of the temple in 1938 to today's 450 cast members in Biblical costumes with a soundtrack. In 1966, Irwin Phelps and Roberta Layton created still tableaux. The resurrection of Christ was timed to coincide with the actual rising of the sun, and spectators arrived as early as 5:00 a.m. to get good seats. Music original to the pageant includes Wanda West Palmers's "Oh, That I Were an Angel" and "Mary's Lullaby" (with words by Bertha Kleinman). Above from left to right are Maurice Bateman, producer, with Edwin Jones and Irwin Phelps, directors, in 1969. Below is a rehearsal with angels standing on the roof of the Visitors' Center. (Above Jaynie Payne; below Arlene Bateman.)

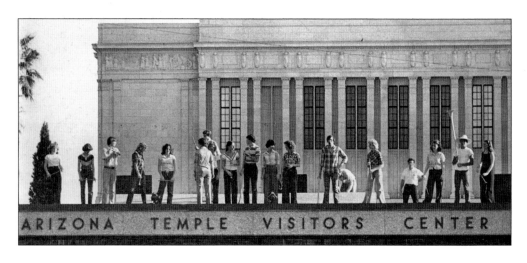

Brian Smith (right) is a High Priest in the 2008 pageant. Barbara Layton, costume designer in 2003, said, "I worked with several Biblical historians, including renowned Carma deJong Anderson, who has a doctorate in Biblical clothing. We tried to make everything we did—down to the smallest accessory—more authentic each year so people could get a taste of what was going on at the time of Christ." (Jeanine Smith.)

The pageant today is titled *Jesus the Christ*. On the soundtrack used after 1977, Joe Dana (left) is the voice of Christ. On the right, Robert Larson portrays Christ in 1982. Originally the directors did not like to acknowledge the identity of the actor portraying Christ because they felt it was a distraction. (Both Jaynie Payne.)

Large numbers of Latter-day Saints have made participation in the Easter pageant a family tradition, with some individuals involved for over 20 consecutive years. Above is a rehearsal, pre-1977, with the stage left, chorus center, and orchestra right. Below are angels and Robert Layton as Jesus Christ. Today the production features a mammoth four-story stage and computerized sound system. It is presented in both English and Spanish over the course of two weeks. Wayne Leavitt, current pageant president, said, "It is presented out of our love for the Savior and a desire to share that with others." (Both Jaynie Payne.)

Five

THIS HOLY HOUSE

In January 1898, James W. LeSueur left Arizona for a mission to Great Britain. He labored in Leeds but then was sent to the Isles of Jersey and Guernsey, where he was given permission to gather genealogical records and visit relatives. In March 1900, he received a telegram of release; his brother Frank had been shot and killed by outlaws near St. Johns. LeSueur wrote, "I missed my brother, Frank, very much. He and I had been like Jonathan and David." Later LeSueur was privileged to see his brother in vision preaching the gospel.

His mission and this vision gave LeSueur a great love of temple work. He wrote, "No sooner was I called to be President of Maricopa Stake in March 1912, than I was in Salt Lake City in April 1912 asking that a temple be erected in Mesa, Arizona." Fund-raising began and sites were considered (including Snowflake and Los Angeles), but construction was delayed by World War I. The site was dedicated in November 1921. Then LeSueur wrote, "Finally in [April] 1922, Apostle David O. McKay [presided at the ground breaking] and I held the plow to throw out the basement and foundation soil and the work began."

During construction, about 25 men were called to act as guides, explaining the purpose of the temple and the gospel plan. Hundreds of tracts were given away, and many copies of the Book of Mormon were sold. LeSueur himself toured many dignitaries, including William Jennings Bryan, Harold Bell Wright, John Galsworthy, and Carrie Chapman Catt.

Additionally, 30 women in the Maricopa Stake (and others in Snowflake and Los Angeles) were called to do genealogical research for members. A library was assembled through a generous donation by Harvey Bush, and classes were held to teach effective research. Memberships in national genealogical societies were taken out, and research trips were made to Denver, Salt Lake City, and Los Angeles. Temple workers were called, particularly from the Maricopa Stake, and when the temple was dedicated, nearly 30,000 people attended.

The impact of the Mesa Arizona Temple cannot be overemphasized, both in the community and on the lives of the people within its district.

Editors of the *Relief Society Magazine* wrote in August 1921, "We are presenting to our readers this month the eagerly expected sketch of the temple to be erected in the near future in Mesa, Arizona." Architects Don C. Young and Ramm Hansen of Salt Lake City used Solomon's Temple as inspiration, and the editors said, "All that was foreshadowed in the Hebrew temple is fulfilled in our temples of today."

On November 28, 1921, Pres. Heber J. Grant formally dedicated the temple site. More than 3,000 people attended. Date palm branches marked the outline of the future temple, and children sang "Shine On," "Jesus Wants Me for a Sunbeam," and "I Want to See the Temple" as they marched around the perimeter throwing flowers. (Mesa Arizona Temple.)

At the site dedication, Anthony W. Ivins said, "These temples do not come spontaneously, but are the result of our own labor and liberality." September 21–26, 1919, was designated Arizona Temple Drive week. James LeSueur said, "Every Latter-day Saint in Arizona is to be visited and given an opportunity to pledge what he will do. Those who are not members will not be solicited, but should any desire to contribute the same will be greatly appreciated." Historian James McClintock told of a Mesa widow, Amanda Hastings, who donated $15 "on behalf of herself and children." Above, a memorial box (including scriptures, newspapers, and McClintock's *Mormon Settlement in Arizona*) is placed in a wall on November 11, 1923; note the pouring of concrete directly below the flag. Below, men are working on the foundation. (Both Mesa Arizona Temple.)

In January 1923, Arthur Price came to Mesa from Salt Lake to be the supervising architect. He immediately began assembling the materials—sand, rock, and cement. He tested concrete mixtures to get the right hardness, and the first pour was in March. The foundation varied in width (approximately 11 feet wide); the walls were 3 feet thick. Eleven months later, the concrete pillars and roof were complete, and the temple was reportedly "the most carefully measured, scientifically constructed, perfectly organized masses of concrete and steel ever constructed into a building . . . a veritable rock of ages, almost as perfect as if cleft by the hand of God." Above, scaffolding is in place as terra-cotta tiles from California are attached to the exterior. Below, the friezes around the top represent people coming from all nations. (Above Mesa Arizona Temple; below photograph by James Hunt.)

The temple dedication program listed these men as the "Arizona Temple Building Committee": from left to right, (first row) James W. LeSueur, John T. LeSueur, and O. S. Stapley; (second row) G. C. Spilsbury, Frank V. Anderson, and John Cummard. Andrew Kimball was also listed as part of this committee, and Frank Pomeroy often served as inspector of the concrete pours. (Mesa Arizona Temple.)

Workmen at the temple posed for this photograph in June 1925. During the last two years of construction, community members were allowed to visit the building seven days a week. Guides provided tours from foundation to roof, and Sundays were particularly busy with sometimes as many as 1,500 visitors. (Mesa Arizona Temple.)

By October 1927, the temple was complete, and a series of dedication services were held over a five-day period. During this time, concerts, dances, and dramas were presented, and two chapels were dedicated. People came from California and Utah by train and from every corner of Arizona by wagon or car. The *Arizona Republican* reported that "most of the available housing space [was] utilized," including homes of members. (Mesa Arizona Temple.)

Pres. Heber J. Grant (fifth from left) gave the dedicatory prayer at a 10:00 a.m. session on Sunday. Attendance was estimated at more than 5,000. Almost all of the General Authorities came from Salt Lake with their families via Los Angeles and/or the Grand Canyon. The railroad company gave special excursion rates for all who wanted to attend. (Mesa Arizona Temple.)

On October 24, 1927, the Papago Indian Ward choir, directed by Thomas Valenzuela, sang for the 6:00 p.m. dedicatory session of the Arizona Temple. Katherine Valenzuela Hunter, who in later years sang internationally, was a soloist. Later choirs from this ward sang at General Conference and many venues in Southern California. (Utah State Historical Society P4.)

With up to three dedicatory sessions held each day, Mesa Fourth Ward was asked to attend the last session on Wednesday morning. Their choir, directed by Earl Lisonbee, sang "Awake and Arise." Earlier services were held for the Snowflake, St. Johns, St. Joseph (Thatcher), Juarez, (Mexico) San Juan (Utah), San Luis (Colorado), Young (New Mexico), and Maricopa Stakes. Children from 6 to 14 years were invited Tuesday evening. (Stephen Phelps.)

The rural setting of the Mesa Temple at its completion is seen in these two photographs. Above, an aerial view from the southwest was photographed in late 1927. The temple lot originally included 40 acres; the fields north and south of the temple were planted in citrus groves in the 1930s. Below is a photograph of uncertain date before houses lined every street. Today this area is known as the Temple Historic District and is a significant example of community planning. The historic buildings include homes of the MacDonald, Sirrine, Killian, Ellsworth, Flake, Stradling, Farnsworth, and Young families, many of which illustrate important architectural styles in Arizona during the first half of the 20th century. (Both Mesa Arizona Temple.)

"Lovely daughters of Benjamin and Rachel Noble" (from left to right, (first row) Myrtle Riggs; (second row) Mary Clark and Alice Jones; (third row) Irene Rowan, Luella Davis, and Lottie King) wrote Joseph Noble, their brother. Clark, speaking at Conference April 1928, said that "the Maricopa Stake Relief Society was asked to contribute $1,000 toward the [temple]." Through bazaars, a penny fund, concessions at the fair, food sales, and cotton picking, they raised enough money to purchase an electric sewing machine and material to make 144 pieces of temple furnishing and donate $500 in cash because the Relief Society women also contributed their best crocheting, tatting, embroidery, and cut work, Clark said, "One sister told me that she had spent three hours a day for seven weeks on the piece that was allotted to her." Below is a rug believed to have been woven for the Arizona Temple by members of the Navajo Nation. (Above Kenneth Noble; below Church History Museum.)

Evan Peterson, in his book *The Ninth Temple: A Light in the Desert*, described two different roles in the temple, temple workers and patrons. James LeSueur saved the photograph above of temple workers while David Udall (seated center in chair) was president. LeSueur dated the photograph as 1938, but Udall was released in 1934. Below, an unidentified couple stands in front of the temple at an unknown date. Peterson wrote that in 2002 there were about 1,300 ordinance workers and 50 sealers at the temple, plus some paid employees and many additional volunteers. (Above AHS/Tucson 12522; below Mesa Arizona Temple.)

Andrew and Helene Shumway moved to Mesa from Snowflake around 1918; they were active in Woodmen of the World but never in the LDS Church. In 1933, when their fifth child, Bonnie (right in the 1940s), was 12 years old, she decided it was time to be baptized. Bonnie gathered up her two younger brothers, Lynn (age 10) and Ben (age 8), and together the three children walked from their home on North Country Club Drive to the temple, knocked on the door, and announced they had come to be baptized. The next Sunday, the trio walked to Mesa Fourth Ward so they could be confirmed. Children from Mesa were often baptized in the temple font, but children from outlying areas were usually baptized in nearby canals. The photograph below is from a missionary serving in southern Arizona (Western States Mission), 1928–1930. (Right Annette Shumway; below Church Archives P4676.)

James LeSueur wrote, "It was thought that on account of the few Saints in Arizona and the great distances in the temple district (from Colorado, New Mexico, Arizona, Old Mexico, Texas, and California) there would be only a small work done in the Mesa Temple." But, looking over records from 1927 to 1939, he said, "Our records during these years were only exceeded by Salt Lake and Logan Temples [which had] 10 to 20 times as many Saints within 50 miles." The first All-Lamanite Conference was held November 6–7, 1945, (above) with about 200 people from the United States and Mexico attending a temple session entirely in Spanish (the first complete session in a non-English language). Below is another Lamanite conference, March 1, 1951; Spencer W. Kimball, Eugene Flake, and Daniel and Beatrice DeLaCruz can be identified. (Church Archives; above P1587, below P4597-1.)

Saints from Mexico came yearly to the temple. They stayed in homes and at the Mezona with a curtain separating the men's and women's sleeping areas; later dormitories with kitchen facilities and a playground were built at the Interstake Center. Missionaries also stopped on their way to Mexico as seen in this 1949 photograph, which includes Sister Ferrell Madsen. (Photograph by Ferrell Farnsworth, Church Archives P4587-6.)

In 1935, Herman and Gertrude Stulz with their four-year-old daughter Naomi traveled from Fullerton, California, to the Mesa Temple. They wrote, "Year after year we journey to this holy House of God." At Christmas (far right), they called Naomi with her dolls a "Young Mother in Israel." (Church Archives; right P524-1, far right P524-2.)

On March 1, 1934, a memorial service was held in Mesa for the Los Angeles Stake genealogical workers who were killed near Wickenburg as they returned to their homes after a week at the temple (clockwise from top left, Sarah Crawford, Rea Haws, Mabel Gowers, Afton Riggs, Genevieve Scadlock, and Elizabeth McArthur). Latter-day Saints in both Arizona and California mourned this automobile accident. (*Genealogical and Historical Magazine.*)

The fathers of both of these authors (and countless others) carried cards bearing this photograph of the Arizona Temple while serving missions in South Africa and eastern Germany. The Articles of Faith were printed on the back, and home addresses helped missionaries and converts maintain contact through ensuing years. (Barbara Lanier.)

ELDER FLOYD LYMAN LEAVITT

South African Mission
Cumorah Main Road
Mowbray C.P.
South Africa

Home Address
234 South Hibbert Street
Mesa, Arizona

In 1952, elder Delbert L. Stapley dedicated the Bureau of Information and Genealogical Library across the street west of the temple. Logan Brimhall (second row, sixth from left) was director, supervising both youth guides (first row) and adults set apart as missionaries. In 1956, the Visitors' Center was moved to its present location north of the temple. (Church Archives P1203-1-2.)

This petroglyph is on display near the reflecting pool between the Visitors' Center and the temple. Found in the San Tan Mountains about 25 miles south of Mesa, it is representative of many such rocks south and west of Mesa, where manganese oxides form a patina that can be chipped away. Nancy Dana, age 10, is photographed here on Easter Sunday 1957. (Nancy Norton.)

In April 1975, the Arizona Temple became the first to be remodeled and rededicated. The temple was closed for a year for the remodeling and addition of an annex. Then it was open for two weeks of public tours; the first day, 16,273 people visited. The crowds were equally large for the dedication (above). Spencer W. Kimball, beloved by Arizonans because many knew him when he lived in the Safford area, was then president of the LDS Church. He attended the original dedication in 1927 as a clerk for the St. Joseph Stake and said, "I sang in the stake choir and we stood on the top of the temple [annex] to sing." Below President Kimball (left) stands with counselors N. Eldon Tanner (center) and Marion G. Romney. (Utah State Historical Society; above C-330.19, left C-330.9.)

Organist Sharon Shields played for the opening session. She told the *Church News*, "I planned it so that when President Kimball came into the room, I would play 'I am a Child of God.' . . . One of the things that made it so special is that my grandfather, Harry L. Payne, was president of the Arizona Temple" from 1944 to 1953. (Utah State Historical Society C-330.6.)

C. Bryant Whiting, president of the Arizona Temple (center, with counselors Egbert J. Brown, left, and Elmer G. Gerber), understood the members' desires to attend the temple again and said, "I will be disappointed if we do not increase [attendance] by 50 percent. . . . This is as near heaven as we can get here on earth." (Utah State Historical Society C-330.37.)

123

Photographing the Arizona Temple with the cactus garden in the foreground is so common that many people are surprised to see lawns when they visit. Thurber Payne wrote, "An interesting cactus garden was planted near the southwest corner of the front lawn. Most of the varieties of the plantings are native to Arizona." (Mesa Arizona Temple.)

The January 1937 snowstorm in Mesa was so unusual that many family albums from this period have images of snowmen in front yards and snow-covered buildings—the high school, churches, homes, and even the temple. The snow lasted nearly a week, and local camera stores nearly ran out of film. (David Johnson.)

The Temple Garden Christmas Light display began with a single star over the temple, as illustrated in this 1942 postcard. Floyd Leavitt remembers being able to see the star from his bedroom window. In 1995, Milo LeBaron, director of the Visitors' Center, and Bill Arnett supervised the installation of more than 500,000 lights and 50 life-sized figures. They extended the time of the display (from Thanksgiving to New Year's Day) and chose to light it rain or shine. LeBaron told the newspaper, "In the Book of Mormon it says, 'Therefore, hold up your light that it may shine unto the world. Behold I am the light which ye shall hold up—that which you have seen me do.' That's why we do it. We want to hold up the light of Christ." (Above Catherine Ellis; below photograph by Newt Kempton.)

Believing in the eternal nature of marriage, Latter-day Saints in Mesa were originally willing to travel the Honeymoon Trail to St. George or take the train (via California) to Salt Lake City so they could be married in a temple. When the Arizona Temple was dedicated in 1927, such long trips were no longer necessary. Then in 2002, a second Arizona temple was dedicated in Snowflake, and in 2008, temples were announced for Gilbert, north Phoenix, and the Gila Valley. The photographs of Floyd Leavitt and LeOla Rogers (left) in 1954 and Nathalia Cuello and Oscar Casares (below) in 2007 represent all such weddings, past and present, performed in the Arizona Temple. (Left Danette Turner; below Adalberto Partida.)

Countless photographs and paintings demonstrate the love Latter-day Saints have for the Mesa, Arizona, Temple. Using a combination of photography and oil, Merlin Ellis produced this painting (above) of the Visitors' Center and temple with Bertel Thorvaldsen's *Christus* as a focal point. The original *Christus* in Copenhagen, Denmark, has been visited by many members and was photographed by missionaries as they were evacuated from Germany in August 1939. This 10-foot copy was added to the Visitors' Center in 1981. At right, Donna and Milo LeBaron, directors of the Visitors' Center from 1994 to 1996, pose at Christmastime with the outstretched hands of Christ above their heads. Many missionaries, converts, and members use similar photographs to remind themselves of their commitment to Jesus Christ. (Above Merlin Ellis; right Jackie Ellis.)

ACROSS AMERICA, PEOPLE ARE DISCOVERING SOMETHING WONDERFUL. *THEIR HERITAGE.*

Arcadia Publishing is the leading local history publisher in the United States. With more than 4,000 titles in print and hundreds of new titles released every year, Arcadia has extensive specialized experience chronicling the history of communities and celebrating America's hidden stories, bringing to life the people, places, and events from the past. To discover the history of other communities across the nation, please visit:

www.arcadiapublishing.com

Customized search tools allow you to find regional history books about the town where you grew up, the cities where your friends and family live, the town where your parents met, or even that retirement spot you've been dreaming about.